Morning has Broken

Morning has broken like the first morning
Blackbird has spoken like the first bird
Praise for the singing
Praise for the morning
Praise for them springing fresh from the Word

Sweet the rain's new fall, sunlit from heaven
Like the first dewfall on the first grass
Praise for the sweetness of the wet garden
Sprung in completeness where His feet pass

Mine is the sunlight
Mine is the morning
Born of the one light Eden saw play
Praise with elation, praise ev'ry morning
God's recreation of the new day

Morning has broken like the first morning
Blackbird has spoken like the first bird
Praise for the singing
Praise for the morning
Praise for them springing fresh from the Word

Eleanor Farjeon

Dedication

To the seven,

in reminder of a

special healing of history

29 June 2021.

'To think that we lived to see this Day!'

Contents

1	*Morning Has Broken*
5	Introduction
6	*Bethsaida*
9	**The Garden Touching Heaven and Earth**
30	Notes
32	Prayer
33	Discussion Questions
34	*Gilead*
37	**Walking the Darkness**
65	Notes
66	Prayer
66	Discussion Questions
67	Blessing
68	Acknowledgments and Attributions
70	From the *Song of Zacharias*

Introduction

'I'm giving you every place where the sole of your foot falls, just as I promised Moses.'

Joshua 1:3 ISV

The Book of Joshua opens with God speaking to Joshua and re-affirming a pledge He'd made previously. He was gifting to the people of Israel, as their irrevocable inheritance, every place where the sole of their feet trod.

This emphasis on the sole of the foot is clearly meant to evoke a covenant and to underline the perpetual aspects of God's bequest. That's because *sole*, in Hebrew, is 'kaph', just as *palm* is — and that's true whether it's the palm of the hand or a frond of a palm tree — and is related to 'kaphar', *make atonement*.

Atonement is *at-one-ment,* the act of bridging division and bringing about oneness. Raising a covenant is essentially a ceremony of creating oneness. We tend to associate the atonement of Jesus solely with His death on the cross. Yet His life was a continual pageant of bridging division and initiating oneness wherever He went.

In the two stories presented in this volume, it's my hope you will see God's promise to Joshua in a new light as we trace the byways Jesus walked. Our world needs healing. And Jesus shows us how to heal deep historical wounds as He follows an ancient path and demonstrates His power to set things right.

In one narrative, Jesus completes the task God gave to Elijah to set up a new government in Samaria — He begins the work of overturning eight centuries of harm that might have been avoided if Elijah had followed God's instructions.

In the second story, which is inspired by the design of John's gospel with its twinned scenes of matching themes, Jesus walks point-to-point along a very significant pathway. He honours the first king of Israel in the process. However much of a surprise it is to realise that Jesus deeply respected Saul's memory, it is much more startling to realise that many of His actions paid homage to some very obscure women. How many of us know of Rizpah, Merab, Michal, Jephthah's daughter and the child-brides of Jabesh Gilead?

It's only when we look at the localities Jesus went, how long He stayed there and where He journeyed to next that we can begin to appreciate the historical parallels in His actions. Jesus did not just honour the heroes of the past, but the almost-invisible individuals too.

Let us open our minds and hearts to see His redeeming work, so we can follow where His feet pass..

Anne Hamilton
Seventeen Mile Rocks
July 2021

BETHSAIDA

Awake, O north wind, and come, O south wind.
Breathe on my garden and spread the fragrance of its spices.

✟— Song of Songs 4:16 BSB —✟

✟— Luke 10:1 NASB —✟

After this the Lord appointed seventy others,
and sent them in pairs ahead of Him to every city.

THE GARDEN TOUCHING HEAVEN AND EARTH

This narrative is told from the perspective of the apostle, James, the son of Zebedee and brother of John

Ask me about fish, I can tell you. Ask me about fruit, different story. That's not to say I'm lacking in familiarity with fruit. Just that I have to admit I'm an expert at catching fish but, when it comes to fruit, my real talent lies in eating it.

I wanted to let you know this upfront because then you'll understand if I blunder about describing the gardens. Because that's what my story is about. Actually I guess that's what everyone's story is all about, now that I come to consider it. The call to return to the Garden. Oops, first blunder. I meant, the call to return to the Gardener.

It all started because my brother and I were friendly with Simon and Andrew from Bethsaida. The town turns up in a significant way later on, so I'd better tell you now what it means: *house of the hunter*. A fitting name. In more ways than one. Simon and Andrew, along with Philip, as well as my brother John and I were all fish-hunters.

Bethsaida was built on the ruins of Geshur — the ancient capital of the territory ruled by Talmai. Yes, the very same Talmai who was David's father-in-law and Absalom's grandfather. Geshur, *bridges*,[1] was indeed the city Absalom fled to after killing the heir-apparent to David's throne — his half-brother, Amnon.

Maybe you know that the prime motivation for that murder wasn't eliminating a rival but the twisted desire for justice after the rape

---

1. Bridges are strangely absent in Scripture. Until the Romans came, they were very rare, and only the apocryphal book of Maccabees mentions a town with a bridge and fortifications named Casphin or Caspin (2 Maccabees 12:13). This town is now a village called Khisfin and is located in the Golan Heights. It is intriguing to note that this singular example of a bridge was in the same area as the long-disappeared kingdom of Geshur.

of the princess Tamar. It was in the long-vanished palace of Geshur that Absalom's obsessive craving for revenge ripened. His brother was just the first to feel the knife of Absalom's judgment. He'd also festered with rage at his father for neglecting gentle, inconsolable Tamar. He was determined to mete out 'justice' for the dishonour his father had done nothing to redress.

Ever feel vengeance brooding in a landscape? Sometimes I sensed it, waiting and wanting, beneath the ground of Bethsaida. There Absalom's conspiracy was conceived and his long-term plans for rebellion were plotted out. David had been hunted for years by Saul without success, and Absalom was determined not to make the same mistakes. When he hunted David down and overthrew his government, he wanted to be sure of victory.

Now, of course, it didn't end well for Absalom — but the point I'm making about him is that Bethsaida has always been associated with the overthrow of government. Can't get away from it — even in such a small thing as its name. Think, after all, right back to the first hunter — he too was a charismatic rebel able to rally others to his cause.

I'd been acquainted with Simon, brother of Andrew, half my life, you know, and not for a single second had I seen in him the ability to step into that mould. I never imagined he had the potential to gather

others around him and overthrow a government. But he came from Bethsaida, so I guess I should have. Because, as the leader of the followers of The Way, he went on to turn the whole world upside down. That was, of course, after he was renamed 'Cephas'.

You know, I could never understand why Jesus chose to appoint him at our head but, the more I think about it, the more I realise how fitting it was. The kingdom of heaven is meant to overthrow every government in every nation in every era, so it makes total sense. Simon, son of Jonah, *the dove*, was summoned to complete the true and unfulfilled calling of Absalom, *my father is peace*, and so bring to pass the destiny of Bethsaida as well.

This is what we're all called to do, you know. To bring to completion unfinished assignments, to unite with Jesus — the One who perfects our faith and brings it to a faultless finale — to heal history, to mend the world, to repair the wounds of the past. In fact, most of the story I'm about to tell you is about how Jesus brought an end to the incomplete missions that should have been completed by two outstanding heroes of our faith. Just to show us all — for future reference — how it should be done.

It was only when I actually met the second of those heroes of the faith as Jesus was about to put the last touches to his unfinished work, that I started to put the pieces together. It finally dawned on me that these two prophets had the same assignments, even though they lived over nine centuries apart.

You're wondering, I suspect, how I could possibly meet two prophets who lived in such different eras. All will be explained.

But first, back to the beginning. If I have to pin the responsibility on anyone for how we all met Jesus, then I'd have to lay it squarely at Andrew's shoulders. It was New Year — Rosh Hashanah — and we'd heard talk of a prophet at Bethany-beyond-the-Jordan. Andrew was keen to head on down there for the festival of Yom Kippur and check it out. It was an attractive idea. Quite apart from satisfying our curiosity about the rumour that, possibly, just possibly, the Elijah-who-was-to-come had emerged in our lifetime, it had the advantage of being a lot closer than Jerusalem. That meant that we could do

something that could be classified as 'holy' for the Day of Atonement without actually having to brave the arrogant sneers of the Samaritans who loathed us with a passion, or the equally arrogant sneers of the Judeans who loathed us with a similar passion. We wouldn't have to go through Samaria or Judea — we could just nip across the Lake, park the boats, hike half a day to Scythopolis, then cross the Jordan and track up the wadi until we found the crowds. Easy.

Yeah, I hate to admit it but we had serious ulterior motives in turning up at Bethany-beyond-the-Jordan for John's baptism of repentance. At least I did. I wasn't looking for the Messiah. I was looking for a way to minimise my time away from the family business. I wanted to get back to fishing as soon as I could. I didn't for a minute imagine my life was about to be overturned and my plans for the future totally upended. I know, I know. You'd think that only genuine believers would respond to the voice in the wilderness crying, 'Repent for the Kingdom of heaven is at hand! Prepare the way for the Lord! Make His paths straight!' We were genuine, but... well, yeah, there were a lot of *buts* mixed in.

We were surprised as we travelled up the valley to the baptismal pools to see a sprinkling of Pharisees in the groups of pilgrims. Their phylacteries were so big and their tzitzit so long, we knew they were the most righteous of all the intensely righteous. 'Why are they here?' Simon whispered. 'What do they have to repent of?'

'Maybe they want answers.' Andrew was staring up at the high rocky walls of the wadi. 'You know, whether or not John is the one prophesied by Malachi — the Elijah-who-is-to-come. This location is a sign, after all. It's where Elijah the Tishbite hid out, just after he started his ministry by announcing the drought to King Ahab.'

He was so earnest I couldn't resist the impulse to tease him. 'You looking for some ravens to swing by with some lunch for you? Like they did for Elijah?'

He made a face at me. My brother John intervened before Andrew could snap a retort back. 'So this is the Brook Cherith?'

Andrew nodded. 'Yes. The brook of *the cut*. The cut of covenant. It's a perfect place to choose when it comes to baptising people who want to proclaim their willingness to return to God through repentance.'

It wasn't long before we came across the pools and soon lost each other in the milling crowds. While Andrew and my brother waited in line to get closer to John, I clambered up over the pink rocks to investigate the higher reaches of the stream. I didn't go all that far before I found a secluded waterfall, overhung with aromatic trees and bordered by medicinal herbs. It made an ideal hide-out. I wondered if I'd found Elijah's refuge — from the days before the brook dried up and he set out for Zarephath. It was a fanciful moment but, even as I thought it, there wasn't the slightest suspicion in my mind I'd just stepped onto the path Elijah had trod and that, one day soon, I too would be heading out in the same direction as Zarephath — to the region of Tyre and Sidon.

I thought about eating the dried fish I had with me but then realised it was still Yom Kippur. I'd never been particularly religious but something about the environs prompted me to keep the fast. I climbed up a rocky pathway near the waterfall and saw Pella in the distance. Then I wandered the clifftop until I found a descent back to the pools. And I don't quite know what made me line up for baptism. But just before the sun set and the Day of Atonement was done, I

slipped into the water at the Baptiser's direction.

I didn't rejoin the others that night. I found a circle of John's disciples around a campfire where I was welcome to dry myself and get warm and, once there, I didn't move. I woke late the next morning, shared my dried fish with a boy and realised I'd committed myself to a new way of living. Unsure of what that meant, I was unwilling to face the others until I'd thought it through. I needed time to myself. So I spent the day watching John and his disciples interact with the Pharisees and the officials from Jerusalem.

I was surprised Andrew wasn't amongst them, to be honest. I didn't see him until just after four in the afternoon. He was looking for Simon. 'Where's John?' I asked. I meant my brother, not the Baptiser.

He caught my meaning straight away. 'He's over there.' He pointed to a rocky outcrop in the distance. A couple of figures were standing on top, silhouetted by the late afternoon sun. 'He'll signal us if the man moves off. But I don't think He will. He said He'd wait. I need to find Simon.'

'What man?' I asked.

'The man the Baptiser was speaking about yesterday. We've spent the day with Him. I want Simon to meet Him.' He looked me up and down, as if assessing how I'd react. I later discovered he moderated his words. 'Don't worry.' His smile was sudden, tentative. 'He's a Galilean.'

So? More than half the crowd was from Galilee. I soon discovered why Andrew was being so mysterious. Once Simon was found and dragged out of a conversation with a couple of oil merchants from Pella, it transpired Andrew wanted us to meet someone he said was the Messiah.

'Which Messiah?' I gave him the full benefit of the fierce hunter scowl I'd perfected for the times when the tax collectors came snooping around the boats. 'Royal Messiah? War Messiah? Priestly Messiah?'

Andrew didn't answer. He just shrugged and insisted we meet Jesus. I still remember the very first words I heard Him say. 'You are Simon, son of Jonah. You will be called *Cephas.*'

Cephas? I wondered. What for? For 'Caiaphas', the high priest? Or for 'kippur', the atonement season we were still in? They were basically the same words, after all.

Exactly two years later, we were to find out. It was again the Day of Atonement, and we were yet again out in a wilderness, and the whole question of the identity of the Messiah was out in the open for once more. And because Simon had declared Jesus to indeed be the Christ, He had finally bestowed that name long-promised: *Cephas.* Or *Peter,* if you prefer.

In the two years leading up to that, we'd become dedicated disciples of Jesus. In fact, to my amazement, He counted me one of the inner circle of three. It wasn't a big deal at first. We'd just followed Him back to Galilee, attended a wedding with Him and then went our separate ways. We all got together again after He turned up at the fishing grounds near Bethsaida and said to Andrew and Simon,

'Come follow Me and I will make you fishers of men.'

It's difficult when you don't know the old language to catch the nuances of what He said. *Fishing* and *hunting* are the same word in Hebrew. Fishers of men, hunters of men: there's no difference. But the ancient echoes in that word, *hunter,* they were hissing at me like fat on a fire. I wondered if Jesus had deliberately evoked them. He was a rabbi, after all, and they often spoke of the sinister tradition about the original hunter of men.

Bethsaida, *the house of the hunter*, might have been associated with a notorious rebel — Absalom, son of David — but he was far from the most infamous in our history. That dubious honour went to the very first huntsman, Nimrod, the leopard-tamer. In constructing eight cities, he was regarded as the first empire-builder.[2] Furthermore, in seeking inhabitants for those cities, he was considered the first 'hunter of men'. His residence, *house of the hunter*, was traditionally thought of as the Tower of Babel.[3]

It was only when we came back to Bethsaida, after I met Elijah, that it became obvious to me what Jesus was doing. Yes, I met Elijah. The one and only original 'troubler of Israel'. The wild, goat-hair-wearing prophet who had never seen death but who was taken up to heaven in a whirlwind. Just after Simon had been renamed Cephas, Jesus

2.
One of these cities was Nineveh where, in a later age, the prophet Jonah was sent to warn the people to repent. Jonah came from Gath Hepher in Galilee (2 Kings 14:25), reminding us that the Pharisees were wrong when they said to Nicodemus, 'Look into it, and you will find that a prophet does not come out of Galilee.' (John 7:52 NIV)

took him and me, along with my brother John, on a trek up a high mountain. There, as a cloud came upon Him and a voice spoke from the majestic Glory, He was transfigured into a dazzling form, more resplendent than the sun. And Moses and Elijah appeared on either side of Him, speaking about the work He was still to accomplish.

Simon often takes the rap for a dumb comment at that particular moment. Truth is, it wasn't such a stupid remark, considering it was the Feast of Tabernacles. Fortunately, none of the accounts of the event record what I was thinking. The only coherent thought that managed to surface from the tumult in my brain was: *how can Moses possibly be here? Has God changed His mind? Didn't He say 'enough' and adamantly refuse to discuss the matter further when Moses asked if he could go to the Promised Land by way of the hill country and Lebanon? So what's Moses doing here in the mountains on the border of Lebanon?*[4]

In retrospect, I think it was because Jesus was fulfilling the Law and also finishing the work of the prophets. He was completing those tasks both Moses and Elijah left undone. I didn't really come to understand that until a week later when we got back to Bethsaida. In the back of my mind I knew Elijah hadn't finished well. Sure, there was always a tendency amongst some scribes and rabbis to set him on a pedestal but, let's be frank, his knees were clay, not just his feet and ankles. I'm not trying to put him down, just trying to inject the right perspective into his life.

3.
Scripture does not record the name of the leader who authorised the building of the Tower of Babel, however long tradition ascribes that role to Nimrod. The tower was made of bricks, not stone, and they may have been white since 'laban' for *brick* is also a word for *white*. A dazzling white tower in the middle of a plain would certainly have attracted people and aided Nimrod's empire-building programme.

4.
'And I pleaded with the Lord at that time, saying, "O Lord God… please let me go over and see the good land beyond the Jordan, that good hill country and Lebanon." But the Lord was angry with me because of you and would not listen to me. And the Lord said to me, "Enough from you; do not speak to Me of this matter again."' Deuteronomy 3:23–26 ESV

You remember the story of how he faced off with the prophets of Baal? He'd come back from Zarephath and gone looking for Ahab, the king of Samaria. It had become a dustbowl after three years without rain. He'd met up with Obadiah, the king's steward, who was extremely unhappy about becoming Elijah's messenger. Ahab had a tendency to shoot the messenger if things didn't work out and Obadiah was deeply concerned Elijah was about to perform another of his vanishing acts. In an effort to reassure him and persuade him to stay where he was, Obadiah told him something of tremendous significance. Holed up in two caves were a hundred prophets, faithful to Yahweh. Obadiah was secretly supplying them with bread and water. This is a critical item of information regarding the task Elijah failed to bring to fruition.

Events moved swiftly once Obadiah contacted the king. A day or so later, Elijah was on top of Mount Carmel confronting the prophets of Baal. It was a spectacular demonstration of divine power, showing Ahab and his court as well as the assembled people of Israel that not one of the four hundred and fifty prophets really has the ear of the 'Cloud-rider' who sends the rain.[5] By the end of the day, fire had descended from heaven onto a stone altar, the prophets of Baal were dead and Elijah had hurtled down Mount Carmel ahead of Ahab's chariot in an attempt to outrace the storm wind plunging out of heaven.

5.
'There is no one like the God of Jeshurun, who rides across the heavens to help you and on the clouds in his majesty.'
Deuteronomy 33:26 NIV

Carmel: the garden. Let that settle in your thoughts. Meditate on it. Let all the storm winds surrounding the word spin into your heart and rest there. A garden on a mountain is a copy of Eden, the jewel-adorned mount of God where the angels walk among the fiery stones. Carmel was a pale copy, yes, of the first cosmic mountain — but still it was by sealed by God's presence as a legitimate one. There are other copies too — other places where the Gardener re-established His government once more.

The storm wind from heaven following the removal of the prophets of Baal was the perfect opportunity to seize the day. Jezebel's power was broken and all Elijah needed to do to change the government was ask Obadiah to usher the one hundred faithful prophets of Yahweh out of the caves and into the court.

Eden was a place of government. Adam and Eve, God's regents, were charged with extending the order and rule of Eden to all the earth. They were appointed as 'shomer' — guardians, keepers, stewards, watchers — called to cultivate fruit trees and create orchards of love, joy, peace, patience, kindness, goodness, faithfulness, gentleness and self-control that would cover the earth.

Samaria, the capital of Ahab's kingdom and the name often given to his nation, is a name derived from 'shomer'. God had plans for Samaria — a future and a hope involving a radical return that would have been no less than a reversal of the fall in Eden. Only first, the government needed to be overthrown — Ahab and Jezebel needed to stripped of their power base: those false prophets who were their cabinet members, congressional representatives and deep state operatives.

Done. It should have been a moment of rejoicing and return. Jezebel was effectively left with nothing but intimidation. But it proved enough.

She issued a death threat. Did Elijah shrug his shoulders and say, 'So? Another one? Your Majesty, much as I'd like to give you preferential treatment, you'll have to join the back of the queue.'

Did he recognise the emptiness of her words? No. He panicked. He did a runner. Fled the kingdom. Pelted down to Beersheba. Met an angel. Ate the angel's food and, in the strength of that sustenance, travelled south for forty days — until he reached another cosmic mountain: Horeb. It too was a place of government: this was the mountain of fire and awe where God had given Moses the law.

As Moses had done before him, Elijah hid himself in a cleft in the rocks and there he experienced a fire, an earthquake, a whirlwind — and a silence. God was not in the earthquake or the wind or the fire, but out of the silence He spoke in a still, small Voice.

It was a rebuke. A gentle rebuke, full of compassion and understanding. But it was still a rebuke. Elijah was moaning on about the people turning against God — when in fact they'd just turned back to Him. He complained that all God's prophets had been slaughtered and that he was the only faithful one left. Now God could have reminded him about those hundred prophets Obadiah was sheltering but He went one better: He told him there were seven thousand in Israel who had not bent the knee. This was a sizeable number, given that it matched the strength of Ahab's army.[6]

Did Elijah realise at that moment how monumentally he'd failed? You see, if those seven thousand had been divided into bands headed up by one of each of the hundred prophets, there would have been seventy in each band.

Seventy. That number speaks loudly and unmistakably of God's purpose. From the time of Babel, seventy has symbolised both the 'number of nations' and the 'number of government' in our culture. God had wanted the wind from heaven that blew down from Carmel

6.
1 Kings 20:15

to be the agency of a new government: bands of seventy taking the good news of change throughout Samaria and teaching the people how to renew the covenant with Yahweh.

And although, because of Elijah's panicked flight, the propitious moment had passed, God still wanted a change of government. And He still wanted Elijah to be part of it. Less to the forefront, sure, but that should have suited Elijah. After all, he'd made it clear he wanted out. He wanted to retire. And God basically agreed. He asked for just three things first: anoint Jehu, anoint Hazael and anoint Elisha. Two new kings and a personal successor. None of these involved a return to Samaria. In fact, Elijah could have simply taken the ancient King's Highway up to Damascus to visit Hazael, then head home by way of Ramoth Gilead where Jehu was stationed, pass the mantle to Elisha and finally put his feet up for as long as he liked.

But did he do as God asked? Concerning Elisha, maybe. If throwing his cloak over him qualifies, then yes. But regarding Jehu and Hazael? No. Years went by, and Elijah procrastinated. More years went by. Through them all, he delayed and dawdled and deferred obedience. He never did anoint either of them. It was only a considerable time after he'd ascended to heaven that one of the sons of the prophets finally anointed Jehu. And although his successor Elisha many years later met Hazael on a journey to Damascus and informed him he would be king, it is not recorded he anointed him.

Jesus told a story once about two sons. One said to his father, 'No, I'm not going to do what you want,' but then changed his mind and did it anyway. The second son said, 'Yes, father, I'm on it right away,' but never did anything at all. I sometimes wondered if the second son in the story was Elijah — the one who started out so well but then gave up. The one who left so much undone and who wasted so many divinely sent opportunities. Elijah defied God — there's no way of softening that reality. He was headstrong and rebellious — and apparently he thought he knew better than God who should be king. His actions seem to indicate that, in his view, Ahab — for all his faults and weaknesses — was a more malleable option than his violent, uncouth battle commander, Jehu. And Ben-Hadad, who was willing to make a treaty with Israel, was a softer option than the brutal Hazael.

Inevitably, another garden came into the picture. Naturally it too was situated on a mountain, and it also involved 'shomer'.

I'm of the view now that, had Elijah not procrastinated so long, the tragedy of this particular garden would never have occurred. Had he appointed the hundred prophets straight after the conflict on Carmel or even if he'd anointed Jehu on his return from Horeb, innocent people wouldn't have suffered. Most people call this garden Naboth's Vineyard, but it's definitely described as a 'kerem', *a garden*, just like Ein Kerem, *the garden spring*, the birthplace of John the Baptist, and similar to Carmel, *the garden mountain*.

Naboth's Vineyard was right next to Ahab's palace on the hill of Samaria. Many centuries later Herod the Great rebuilt the city and named it Sebaste in honour of Caesar Augustus. It's no coincidence John the Baptist was executed in the fortress there. Like Naboth, he was killed on a woman's orders despite the reluctance of the reigning king to do away with him. This taps right back to Elijah's primal fear — that despite a relationship with Ahab that verged almost on friendship — Jezebel would make good on her threat. Like John's interactions with Herod, Elijah's talks with Ahab were both amicable and challenging. Elijah prophesied to Ahab that dogs would lick Jezebel's remains by the wall of Jezreel — which, in the fullness of time, turned out to be Naboth's Vineyard. And, hearing a similar fate pronounced for himself, Ahab repented.

Years went by, and Jehu finally came to the throne. When he did, Jehu reminded his officer Bidkar that they'd been riding along behind Ahab's chariot when he'd received the prophecy about Jezebel meeting a gruesome end in the vegetable patch — the garden that had been Naboth's Vineyard. Since Elijah delivered that word, he'd obviously seen Jehu in person but let the opportunity pass.

I mention all this because I'm no different. In another garden, I was especially privileged to be selected as a 'shomer', a guardian, a watchman, a steward, a keeper — but I couldn't even watch and pray for one hour. Elijah might have panicked after the great triumph on Mount Carmel, but it's important to remember panic and rejection are inextricably entwined. Elijah might not have rejected God as

Jezebel did, but he rejected the government of God. And he went on rejecting the government of God — right up, I suspect, until the moment I met him on the mountain. When I too began rejecting the government of God. Because, unlike Elijah, I couldn't wait to be part of it. I was impossibly eager to take my royal seat next to the Messiah as His right-hand man.

As I said, there are many copies of Eden — the mount of God with the garden watered by streams of living water. Some are divinely sanctioned and some are imposters. Those that are places of light and healing are called to foreshadow the redemptive work of Jesus. And those that are dark and deceptive — well, they too are called to exactly the same task! Maybe 'foreshadow' is no longer the right word. How do I explain His finished work that still mysteriously looks forward to its completion in the outworking of our lives?

Of all the accursed localities in history, few compared to the mountain where the angels themselves threw maledictions at one another as they bound themselves with oaths to seek mates from amongst the daughters of humanity. Snow-bound, on our northern border, it was renowned as the mountain where the seventy 'young lions', the sons of the goddess Asherah, had their palaces and met together in assembly. Yes, seventy again. Here the spirit-rulers of the nations met in convocation, even as they warred amongst themselves.

There was an old prophecy that God Himself would one day stand up and denounce this 'assembly of the gods' where corruption was so rife. He would decree mortality and pronounce death over these Watchers who had sought to unite themselves with the flesh of mortal women. He would furthermore declare the coming of justice and mercy.[7]

The last thing that ever crossed my mind when Jesus called on Simon as well as my brother and me to venture up the mountain was that we were walking headlong into that prophecy. There we were, stepping on and off herb-bordered paths that led to different temples and shrines, puffing with the altitude, our breath becoming misty in the icy air. Jesus was being mysterious, but there wasn't anything particularly abnormal about that. It was all so informal we weren't aware we'd stepped into another realm and into the Lord's Council chambers until Elijah and Moses appeared. I think John stuttered, 'S-s-should we take off our s-s-sandals?' but later he couldn't remember speaking at all. We could only remember Simon's inane comment about building tabernacles. Fact is, we were all pretty much reduced to stunned fish. And that was even before the Glory swirled in and identified Jesus as His Beloved.

Despite being terror-stricken with awe, the implications of what we'd witnessed and where we'd been finally dawned on us as we were descending the mountain. The time of the principalities of the nations was over. Over. Their reign was at an end. The Messiah was here! He was not only the King of Israel but King of kings — He been acknowledged as the Son of the Most High. He was Lord of all the world! And we, incredibly, yes we — my brother and I, two fish-hunters of Galilee — we were His chosen councillors!

By the time we got back to Bethsaida, we had it sorted in our minds: one on His right hand, one on His left, Simon Peter as His chamberlain at the door. We could understand now what was happening even as it happened: in Bethsaida, the ancient kingdom of Geshur, the landscape where Absalom's revolt was first conceived, Jesus had begun an incredible reversal of the very essence of what rebellion meant.

While Absalom was the son of David who tried to overthrow the government, Jesus was the Son of David who had begun implanting

7.
Psalm 82.

the government of heaven into the land. Not content with refashioning the revolution of Absalom, He was also upending the work of Nimrod, the first man in Scripture to be named a 'rebel' and the original 'hunter of men'.[8] The empire Jesus wanted to build was in complete contrast to Nimrod's with its centrepiece Tower of Babel. He was ushering in the Kingdom of God with its gospel of repentance and restoration.

The wind from heaven was stirring again. The cloud as small as a man's hand was forming — but did we notice? No, we were looking the other way. Our understanding of the work of Jesus was faulty beyond imagining. Sure of our coming status, we were still thinking politically. We'd told our suspicions privately to our mother and she was less sure about Jesus' intentions than we were. But she figured there was one way to be sure: put Him on the spot where He had to make a public declaration about our rank in His government.

We were still smarting from the humiliation we suffered when she bailed Jesus up in front of the other disciples, when — well, we thought it couldn't get worse. But it did. We sank even further into the mire.

The problem was simple: the dazzling image of Jesus in His transfigured glory was still in our minds as we headed down through Samaria. And as one community after another rejected Him, we were indignant. He was the liberator, the prophesied one who would save us — and the time of His unveiling was fast approaching. That's

8.
It is interesting to note that Nimrod was the first cousin of Sidon, whose name also means *hunter* or *fisher*.

what we'd realised on the mountain: He was about to appoint a new government. We'd seen Elijah and knew we were on-track to finish the legislative assignment he'd never completed. We'd seen Moses and recognised we were called to partner in establishing new commandments for the fulfillment of the Kingdom.

So we were incensed that the Samaritans didn't recognise Jesus. In fact I was so offended I wanted to use my new-found authority to call down fire from heaven to show those mixed-breed ingrates just who they were dealing with. But Jesus rebuked us. He told me off and John as well, calling us 'Boanerges', *sons of thunder*. No one, other than Simon, understood the real deeps of that reprimand. After all, we'd been to the Mountain of Assembly where the angel-shepherds of the nation held their court. And where the Voice of the Glory had said of Jesus: *'This is My beloved Son, in whom I am well-pleased.'*

But what was Jesus saying by calling us *sons of thunder*? Not only did He imply Yahweh was far from well-pleased with our attitude but He indicated we didn't even belong to the Lord. Instead He told us that we served Yahweh's rival — the king over the seventy young lions, Baal-Hadad, the Voice of the Thunder.

Of course, Baal-Hadad. Just as Ahab had a treaty with Ben-Hadad, so we had a spiritual agreement with the power behind that long-defeated throne.

We were devastated. Humbled. John had been so secure in the love of Jesus, he was crushed for days. We hadn't thought ourselves part of the foolish and perverse generation that Jesus had censured back at Pan's temple. We'd let ourselves off the hook because we hadn't been part of the attempts to heal the epileptic boy whose father had

taken him to Caesarea Philippi looking for a cure. The mountaintop experience had swelled our pride to such a degree we'd thought ourselves exempt from the accusation.

But, there in Samaria, Jesus made it clear how shaky our allegiance to the Living God really was.

But still — but *still* — He gave us another chance. And *still* again. I look back now and wonder at how ignorant we were regarding the pit harbouring our pride. It was abyss-deep. And I also wonder just how often Elijah received another chance. God had wanted to change the government of Samaria back in his days but it took Jesus to do it.

And when He did it, seventy individuals were of course involved again. As we were heading down to Samaria, Jesus appointed seventy messengers and sent us out to announce the coming of the Kingdom. We'd had a trial run previously with just twelve of us, but once the seventy were sent out to heal the sick and preach the Good News, our assignment became unmistakably *governmental* in nature.

If a town doesn't accept you, Jesus said, simply wipe the dust from your feet and leave. John and I felt even more shattered with that instruction. See *dust,* for us, symbolises *resentment*. Leave your resentment and indignation behind was basically what He was saying. Let it testify against the people that they refused the coming of the King's messengers. We were called to usher in a new legislative assembly: one whose first law was *love God* and whose second was *love your neighbour as yourself*.

John and I were broken by that time. We felt so ashamed and inadequate. But Jesus works best, as we should have remembered from the feeding of the people outside Bethsaida, when He can take

and bless and break and share. He'd taken us and blessed us and broken us and now He was sharing the Good News through us with the people of Samaria.

And miracles happened. It wasn't just that people were healed. Demons submitted to us in Jesus' name. And He said to us: *'I saw Satan fall like lightning from heaven. Behold, I have given you authority to tread on snakes and scorpions, and over all the power of the enemy. Nothing will harm you. Nevertheless, do not rejoice that the spirits submit to you, but rejoice that your names are written in heaven.'* [9]

If we hadn't had the experience of being crushed, we might have misunderstood the nature of the authority He was giving to us. Because no one was looking for a Messiah who would teach His people how to turn the epic failures of history into monumental successes by simple obedience. Without the trampling, we'd have understood that authority as the right to *make* the Law, not as the delegated power to *uphold* the Law.

Jesus had come to destroy the works of the enemy and our part in it was to uphold the new commandment: *love one another as He loved us.*

9.
Luke 10:18–20 NIV

That is how He expected us to mend the world and change the government. That is how He wanted to bring about a return to the garden on the cosmic mountain — to reverse the fall. The human race had been dispossessed of a rightful inheritance in Eden, but Jesus had come to restore it. Not politically, as we'd mistakenly thought, but relationally.

It wasn't until John and I, along with Peter, were present in another garden on another mountain that we had any idea what the terrible cost of restoration was going to be. There, as Jesus prayed for the cup to pass from Him, we failed once again. He is not called the Author and Finisher of our faith metaphorically. He literally does complete the assignments we have left undone. But He wants us to work with Him to achieve the mending of the world.

That's why He sent His storm wind out of heaven — so that all of us can bring in His government with its garden of love and peace.

Notes

I once had a dream about wandering the back corridors of heaven. I think I was looking for a library when I was suddenly accosted by two angels. 'Just the person we wanted to see,' one said as he grabbed me by the arm. 'Quickly, come and judge this case.'

'I can't possibly do that!' I protested as they hustled me into a vacant courtroom and escorted me to a judge's bench.

The moment I sat down I was instantly stripped of all ability to recognise the meaning and significance of voice level, facial expression, body language or accent. All the subtle clues that come from different postures and gestures, cadences and inflections of tone, the carriage of a person, the emotional aura they exude — gone. In a flash. I hadn't been aware how much I used these skills until they were flattened into non-existence.

A man was brought into the courtroom. Later, when my ability to discern body language and facial expression returned, I realised he was both furious and horrified. His worst nightmare had come to pass. He was about to be judged by... a *woman*. Fortunately I didn't have to open the case because he announced, 'I shouldn't be here. I can say, "Jesus is Lord."'

This isn't so hard, I thought. *All that's needed is a simple check*. 'That's fantastic. I just need to clarify one point. This "Jesus" you say is Lord, could you be a bit more specific? Perhaps you could say "Jesus of Nazareth is Lord" just so we can be sure it's the same Jesus that we're talking about.'

'Yes, I can do that.' If my other senses were on-line, I'd have recognised the seething scorn and hostility edging his voice. I'd have registered the ramrod stiffness of his back and the barely concealed scowl. But when you've got nothing but words, that's what you go with: words, and words alone.

I waited for the man to get around to doing what he said he could, but he was silent. 'So,' I said, 'can you please repeat your statement about Jesus being Lord and add something to identify the Jesus you're referring to.'

'I told you I could do that.'

'It doesn't have to be "of Nazareth", if you think that's not specific enough. You could pick something from one of the Creeds — 'suffered under Pontius Pilate'; 'born of the virgin Mary'. If you don't think Mary was a virgin, pick something else. We're not saved by doctrine, but by grace through faith. My preference would be for some statement about the resurrection, but it can be whatever you like.'

'Yes, of course, I can say any of that.'

I waited. Silence.

'Maybe I've haven't explained the problem here very well. There are counterfeiting spirits who call themselves "Jesus". So I just like to be clear which Jesus you have a relationship with and who is your lord.'

'But I've told you.'

'You've told me you can say any of the statements I've suggested but you haven't actually made a declaration out loud of any of them. Perhaps you *can* but you haven't.' I stopped and stared into his eyes. 'And the truth is that, if I asked you to repeat word-for-word after me, "Jesus of Nazareth is Lord," you couldn't actually do it, could you?'

I watched the man's face crumble in sudden horror as he realised the truth. At that moment, all those senses I'd been stripped of flooded back in an instant. I recognised his accent, knew his nationality, grasped the confused anger and passive aggression behind his demeanour.

The angels took hold of him and led him away.

I mention this dream because a similar kind of emotional flat-lining is a feature of the Scriptural record. With just a few notable exceptions, the historical stories are told in a dry, flat way. When we've had our taste for adventure or romance whetted by movies or page-turning fiction, it's hard to come to grips with a factual viewpoint that's more like a report summary than a novel. But the value of this style is that we are encouraged to judge the characters by their words and deeds, not by the persuasive skill of the writer. There is no concerted attempt to convince us to take one side in a conflict — yet our human nature and our cultural forms of story-telling naturally lure us into creating 'heroes' and 'villains' and then judging their motivations accordingly.

Yet the people whose lives are detailed in Scripture don't fit neatly under those labels. Even the best of them are complex souls, dappled with brilliantly piercing light and intense darkness. Elijah, as we've seen in this story, spent the latter part of his career defying God. Moses couldn't overcome his fear of the threshold. They were great men but they were tragically flawed.

Nevertheless their stories are — ultimately — an incomparable encouragement. What Elijah was unable to face in his own strength, he was able to do with Jesus by His side. And what Moses was unable to face in his own strength, he was able to do with Jesus by His side. The healing of history is impossible in our own strength, but with Jesus by our side, the upside-down rightside-up world of the Kingdom of Heaven is completely within our grasp.

Prayer:

Heavenly Father, I call on Your unfailing mercy. Grant to me the grace to finish the race well. Not because I deserve it but because Your lovingkindness and faithfulness are new every morning. Do not allow me to be disqualified from fulfilling my calling by allowing my fears to rule me. Do not allow me to be disbarred from my destiny because I can't bring myself to agree with Your ideas and choices. Help me to lay hold of the next chance You give me. Put Your strong and mighty hand over mine and keep it clasped to the opportunities You provide.

Jesus of Nazareth, I ask You to be the Finisher of my faith. You are its Author, but I ask You to help me complete the task for which I need strength far beyond my own.

Holy Spirit, grant to me wisdom and understanding, counsel and might, knowledge and reverential fear of the Lord so that I may align my mind ever more closely with that of Christ, and in Him accomplish the purpose He has created me to fulfill. Lead me and guide me, showing me the ways You want me to partner with You to accomplish the healing of history for my family, my local church, my city, my state, my nation.

In the name of Jesus, whose footsteps mark the path for us to follow.

Amen

Discussion Questions:

(1) Is it uncomfortable to look at Moses and Elijah and realise they rejected God? What does that tell us about the culture of heroism our society promotes?

(2) We are encouraged to be rugged individualists and to believe that private rebellion has no impact on those around us. What were the consequences of the behaviour of Moses and Elijah for the society in which they lived?

(3) Are there areas in your own life where you now recognise you've been avoiding God's call to heal hearts, homes and history? What can you learn from Moses and Elijah about how to change?

All the valiant men arose, and went all night, and took... their bones,
and buried them under the tamarisk-tree in Jabesh, and fasted seven days.

1 Samuel 31:12 ASV

John 10:40 BSB

Then Jesus went back across the Jordan to the place
where John had first been baptising, and He stayed there.

Walking the Darkness

This narrative is told from the perspective of the apostle Thomas, called the Twin.

My name is Thomas, called the Twin. Already I suspect you're thinking that my story is about faith overcoming doubt. I wouldn't want you to be disappointed, so before we get too much further, I suggest you cast aside such preconceptions. My story is instead about twins. It's about pairs and parallels, mirrors and matches, correspondences and counterparts.

Yes, it's about people and places with the same names, events with the same details, miracles with the same theme. It's about Bethany and Bethany-beyond-the-Jordan, Elijah and the Elijah-who-was-to-come, Salem and Jerusalem, Jebus and Jabesh Gilead, Beth Horon the Upper and Beth Horon the Lower, the shadow of Death and the shadow of Blindness.

Be warned: this is also a story about women and the high esteem in which my rabbi held them. There are so many women from the past who shoot into the record of Scripture like a meteor, blaze intensely for a moment and are gone. But Jesus didn't forget them: to my great surprise, He honoured the famous ones like Esther and Rachel and also the obscure ones like Sheerah, Merab and Michal, Jephthah's daughter and the women of Jabesh Gilead.

Winter was upon us when we went down to Jerusalem to celebrate Hanukkah, the festival of lights. Although it's not one of the seasonal feasts appointed by the Lord, it's always held a special place in the hearts of all Jewish people. It commemorates an immense victory

over foreign oppressors and so, from year to year, it rekindled in us a secret flame of hope. Would this be the season of the Messiah's unveiling? How much longer would it be before he emerged and drove back the armies of Rome — smashing them just as Judah Maccabaeus, *the hammer*, did at Emmaus and on the Ascent of Beth Horon when he defeated the superior forces of the Seleucids?

Sure, the first Hanukkah had been almost two hundred years ago. Still, through celebrating the miracle when the oil multiplied to keep the temple lights burning for over a week, we kept alive the dream of freedom's return. But instead of a restoration and re-dedication, as at the first Hanukkah, the dream began to fraying into a nightmare. The lights, instead of burning brighter to shine on the Messiah, were being snuffed out one by one.

We were walking the streets of Jerusalem when we saw a man born blind. That started a spirited discussion and we asked Jesus, 'Rabbi, who sinned, this man or his parents, that he was born blind?'

Jesus answered, 'Neither this man nor his parents sinned, but this happened so that the works of God would be displayed in him. While it is daytime, we must do the works of Him who sent Me. Night is coming, when no one can work. While I am in the world, I am the Light of the World.'

While the rest of the disciples tried to stifle their gasps, I jerked around, desperately hoping there were no Roman soldiers within earshot. *Light of the World?* That was a title of Mithras, a favourite godling of the legions. Imported from Persian religion and now worshipped from one end of the Roman Empire to the other, Mithras was allegedly 'the invincible Sun' whose birthday was three days after the winter solstice.

Jesus had this unfortunate habit of purging His group of followers by making outrageous claims. A vast number of disciples left Him after He called Himself the 'Bread of Heaven'. In lots of ways I was surprised anyone was left. It crossed my mind to turn away too. See, the 'Bread of Heaven' is not only a title of the dying-and-rising harvest deity Tammuz but is also, as anyone familiar with the prophecy of Ezekiel knows, totally forbidden to all loyal worshippers of The Name. In the end, I wasn't sure about what Jesus said but decided that I'd see it through His eyes: which seemed to be that He was stripping Tammuz of a stolen title.

Right, I figured, *so now it's the turn of Mithras.* Thankfully, no one but the blind man was listening in. And better still, Jesus sent him away. Told him to go wash in the Pool of Siloam. *Disaster averted,* I thought to myself. *The only witness has been taken care of.*

That turned out to be such a foolish thought. A couple of hours later, we were eating at one of our favourite inns when we started to hear rumours of what had happened to the man. Who was, according to every report, definitely no longer blind. He'd been hauled up for questioning before the Pharisees. And so had his parents. They'd had a rugged time of it. The Pharisees simply refused to believe the simple truth and eventually, exasperated, they threw the man out, heaping him with insults and curses on the way.

The moment Jesus heard this, He left His meal unfinished and went to find the man. A group of Pharisees were trailing the poor beggar around.

'Do you believe in the Son of Man?' Jesus asked.

'Who is He, Sir?' he replied. 'Tell me so that I may believe in Him.'

'You have already seen Him,' Jesus answered. 'He is the One speaking with you.'